Original title:
Wistful Cues Over the Fae Hill

Copyright © 2025 Swan Charm
All rights reserved.

Author: Paulina Pähkel
ISBN HARDBACK: 978-1-80563-109-5
ISBN PAPERBACK: 978-1-80564-630-3

Beneath the Boughs of Silenced Time

Beneath the boughs, shadows fall,
Whispers of secrets, echoing call.
Time stands still, in quiet grace,
Memories linger, in this sacred place.

Each leaf a story, spun with care,
Of laughter and tears that weave through air.
The dance of the past, a spell so sweet,
In the heart of the woods, where time and silence meet.

A Reverie Rendered by the Breeze

The breeze carries tales from a time untold,
Of dreams whispered softly, in twilight's fold.
A reverie woven with threads of hope,
Guiding lost souls, helping them cope.

The scent of the blossoms, fragrant and pure,
Awakens the heart, offers a cure.
In shadows that linger, the sunlight gleams,
As we dance to the music of soft, stolen dreams.

Glades of Glistening Forgotten Sorrows

In glades where the light, like diamonds, plays,
Forgotten sorrows tread in a haze.
Each droplet of dew, a story concealed,
A sorrowful heart left unhealed.

The whispers of wind, a soft lament,
In the hush of the night, so much is sent.
Every glimmering tear sings of the past,
While shadows of memory around us are cast.

Dreaming Under the Starlit Canopy

Beneath the stars, where wishes take flight,
We find solace in the quiet night.
Each twinkle a promise, each shimmer a dream,
In this sacred moment, all feels supreme.

The canopy stretches, vast and divine,
Embracing our hopes, a lattice of time.
As we whisper our secrets to night's gentle ear,
Dreaming together, with nothing to fear.

The Sigh of a Distant Forest

In twilight's grasp, the shadows weave,
A forest sighs, the night believes.
Beneath the boughs, old secrets sleep,
Where whispers dance and secrets creep.

Moonbeams filter through the trees,
A gentle touch, a soft cool breeze.
The nightingale begins to sing,
Her melody, a hidden spring.

With every rustle, spirits play,
In sacred light, they softly sway.
Echoes of time in leaves' embrace,
The forest keeps its ancient grace.

Stars above, like silver threads,
Weave pathways where the mind now treads.
In every sigh, a story told,
A tapestry of green and gold.

With every breath, the woods awake,
In tranquil dreams, the leaf turns flake.
A heart within this realm does find,
A home where nature's soft aligned.

Memory Carried on the Heartbeat of the Earth

Beneath the soil, the roots entwine,
Whispers of ages in silence refine.
Each heartbeat of earth tells a tale,
Of life once lived, of love not frail.

A river flows with ancient might,
Carving paths through fading light.
Memories drift on the gentle tide,
Where echoes of laughter abide.

Mountains rise like giants old,
Guardians of stories yet to be told.
The winds carry voices, soft and clear,
Reminding us of those who were near.

In twilight's glow, the shadows embrace,
Time unravels with delicate grace.
Each step we take, a dance in the sand,
Where footprints blend with the timeless land.

The heartbeat of the earth goes on,
In every whisper, a memory's drawn.
With each heartbeat, life intertwines,
In the tapestry of fate, each thread shines.

Treading Softly on Shimmering Leaves

In the hushed woods, where magic stirs,
I tread softly, where silence whirs.
Leaves sparkle like jewels in the light,
Each step a dance, each step feels right.

Dappled sunlight through branches falls,
The forest breathes, the stillness calls.
Squirrels dart and shadows play,
In this enchanted, timeless sway.

A rustle whispers secrets old,
Nature's lore in emerald gold.
With every crunch beneath my shoe,
A tale untold in morning dew.

I pause and listen, heartbeats blend,
With every sound, a message sends.
The breeze carries the scent of pine,
Awakening something deep and divine.

In this realm of dreams and sighs,
I find the truth where starlight lies.
Treading softly on shimmering leaves,
My spirit dances, my heart believes.

The Fae's Gift of Silent Laughter

In twilight's glow where secrets nest,
The fae invite to a merry jest.
With silent laughter, they play unseen,
In the realms of magic, the air grows keen.

They weave their spells with a twinkle bright,
In the heart of shadows, pure delight.
Each giggle floats on the midnight breeze,
Tickling leaves on dreaming trees.

In moonlit glades, they twirl and spin,
Their laughter a melody, soft and thin.
While stars above join in their mirth,
The world below feels the fae's rebirth.

With every flutter of wings in flight,
They scatter dreams in the pale moonlight.
A gentle sigh escapes the air,
Promises whispered, with secrets to share.

So linger long where faeries thrive,
In the magic where the heart's alive.
For in their midst, we find pure bliss,
In the silent laughter that we might miss.

The Allure of Hidden Doorways

In shadows deep where secrets dwell,
A door awaits, a whispered spell.
With ivy's grip and time's embrace,
It beckons forth in silent grace.

Old wooden beams, where stories sleep,
Through cracks and creaks, the memories seep.
A flicker bright, a call from deep,
To find the magic we seek to keep.

The latch is worn, the handle cold,
Each speck of dust has tales untold.
With timid hands, we push and pry,
To chase the wonders hidden nigh.

Beyond the veil of mundane life,
A world awaits, free from strife.
With every step, the heart's delight,
To dance with dreams in timeless night.

So dare yourself to cross that line,
For hidden doors lead to the divine.
In every heart, a key resides,
To unlock worlds where magic hides.

Fading Footsteps on Overgrown Paths

In tangled woods where shadows play,
Faint footprints linger, fade away.
Each step a tale, a whisper soft,
Of journeys taken, dreams aloft.

The bramble thick, the mossy stone,
Still echoes of the heart's lone moan.
A winding route, once clear and bright,
Now cloaked in dusk, a fleeting sight.

The birds still sing, the leaves still dance,
Yet every path holds its own chance.
To wander lost, to find anew,
The faded trails that once we knew.

Through fog and mist, a breath of air,
The quiet places, the secrets rare.
With every turn, the heartbeats pound,
In search of what might yet be found.

So grasp your courage, tread with care,
These paths may lead you anywhere.
For in the fading, stories weave,
A magic found in hearts that believe.

An Offering of Petals to the Wind

A gentle breeze, a soft caress,
Collecting dreams, I must confess.
With petals bright, a tribute fair,
To nature's breath, a fragrant prayer.

Each color speaks of joy and pain,
Of laughter shared, of love's refrain.
With every toss, my heart takes flight,
To soar on wings of pure delight.

As blossoms twirl, they weave a tale,
Of summer's warmth and winter's veil.
In moments fleeting, beauty grows,
In whispered secrets only roses know.

So let them dance upon the air,
These fragile gifts beyond compare.
A sacred bond with earth and sky,
An offering made as time goes by.

For in the wind, our hopes reside,
And through the petals, love won't hide.
With every breath, the world shall see,
The timeless beauty meant to be.

Glimpses of Magic Beneath the Oak

Beneath the oak where shadows twine,
The whispers flow like aged wine.
With roots that delve in secrets deep,
The magic stirs from ancient sleep.

In dappled light, the fairies play,
As sunlight fades to end of day.
Each rustling leaf a soft refrain,
Of stories lost and found again.

The bark is etched with years gone by,
Of laughter shared and silent sighs.
With every breeze a secret sways,
In this enchanted, timeless space.

So gather round, oh friends so dear,
For here, the unseen is quite near.
In every nook, a tale unknown,
Of love and loss, of seeds once sown.

So linger long in twilight's hue,
Where magic lives anew for you.
For in the oak, a heart will find,
The glimpses of what's left behind.

Luminescent Wishes in the Evening Air

In twilight's grasp, the stars ignite,
Whispers of dreams take gentle flight.
The moon a pearl, hung high and bright,
Guides the hearts through shimmers of night.

Soft shadows dance on the silken grass,
As fireflies spin in a glowing mass.
Each flicker tells of moments that pass,
While wishes drift like the evening glass.

The breeze carries tales from afar,
Secrets entwined with each twinkling star.
With every breath, believe who we are,
In this enchanting, celestial bazaar.

The night unfolds with a wistful tune,
As starlit paths lead to dreams in bloom.
Embrace the magic in the cool of June,
For every wish sings a hopeful rune.

So let your heart float on the air,
Like luminescent wishes, rare and fair.
In the evening's cradle, with love to share,
We chase the dreams that linger, and dare.

Secrets Etched in Nature's Canvas

Beneath the leaves, a story hides,
In each bark, where time abides.
Nature's whispers, the world confides,
In shaded groves where magic rides.

The petals sigh with colors bright,
Each hue a tale of day and night.
Branches weave in morning light,
As secrets dance within our sight.

Rivers murmur with ancient verse,
In crystal flows, they softly terse.
The wind a gentle universe,
Sings of love, both kind and fierce.

Among the roots, where shadows thrive,
Lies the pulse of all that's alive.
With every heartbeat, we derive,
The stories that the earth can give.

So wander deep through this alive art,
Embrace the wonders that nature imparts.
For in each petal, leaf, and dart,
There lies a truth that fills the heart.

Threads of Longing Through Ancient Boughs

In ancient woods where silence grows,
Beneath the boughs, a longing flows.
Each whisper shared, the soft winds' prose,
Holds the tales that time bestows.

The roots entwine like fingers clasped,
In nature's heart, each moment grasped.
Dreams take flight as shadows rasped,
Through winding paths where echoes masked.

The sunlit glades, a tapestry bright,
Weaving the past with threads of light.
In forest depths, with pure delight,
Longing entwines with each flight.

As twilight drapes its velvet cloak,
The ancient boughs begin to choke.
Yet still, we hear the words unspoke,
In every sigh, a silent joke.

So linger here amidst the trees,
Feel the pulse of the woodland breeze.
For in this longing, hearts find peace,
Threads of whispers never cease.

Flickers of Hope in the Dappled Light

Sunbeams break through the leafy dome,
In dappled light, we find our home.
A myriad of dreams begins to roam,
Flickers of hope where hearts can comb.

With every step on the forest floor,
Life whispers softly, 'Seek evermore.'
Among the shadows, we dare explore,
Finding the treasures that roots restore.

Petals unfurl, alive and bold,
Tales of the heart in colors told.
In nature's bounty, secrets unfold,
Flickers of stories that never grow old.

The brook laughs sweetly, a melody pure,
With glimmers of joy, of love once sure.
Every ripple brings hope to endure,
In this enchanted world, we find our cure.

So let the light guide your weary feet,
In the dappled glow where shadows meet.
Each flicker, a promise, sound and sweet,
Shall carry our dreams on life's soft beat.

Gossamer Threads of Time Unraveled

In the quiet glades, shadows play,
Entwined in the dance, of night and day.
Where whispers echo in soft refrains,
Gossamer threads weave joys and pains.

The clock ticks slow, as memories sway,
Starlit moments, like wisps in the fray.
Each heartbeat counts, a timeless rhyme,
Unraveled secrets of forgotten time.

Beneath the vault of indigo skies,
Dreamers wander, where the magic lies.
Every choice, a stitch in the seam,
Life's fragile tapestry, woven of dream.

Through the years, the past may fade,
Yet embers of love never truly jade.
For in the twilight, hope finds a way,
As gossamer threads weave night into day.

Embrace the journey, let spirits fly,
In the web of time, we learn to try.
For in each moment, a treasure we find,
Gossamer threads of the heart entwined.

Hearts Entwined in the Faery Light

In glimmering glades where the faeries play,
Hearts entwined in the golden ray.
With laughter soft as a lover's sigh,
A magical world where spirits fly.

Beneath the boughs of ancient trees,
Whispers flow with a gentle breeze.
Magic brews in a bubbling brook,
While enchanted tales from the darkness look.

In the heart's chamber, secrets reside,
Where dreams awaken, and hopes abide.
Each flicker of light, a promise kept,
In faery realms where love has leapt.

As dusk settles with a silken thread,
Colors blend where the wild heart led.
A tapestry woven in every glance,
In faery light, we dare to dance.

So take my hand in the twilight glow,
Together we'll wander where wishes flow.
For in the night, our spirits ignite,
Hearts entwined in the faery light.

A Serenade for Dreams Unbound

In the hush of night, dreams take flight,
A serenade calling, soft and bright.
Each note a wish, a journey begun,
In the realm of stars, we chase the sun.

With every whisper, the moonlight sings,
Unraveling wishes on silken wings.
In shadows deep, our fears release,
As dreams entwine, we find our peace.

The world outside fades, a distant roar,
Within our hearts, there's so much more.
With every heartbeat, a story unfolds,
A serenade cherished, as time beholds.

Through valleys vast, and mountains high,
We seek the truth in the boundless sky.
In the quiet sighs and the gentle sound,
We dance to the rhythm, dreams unbound.

So let us wander from dusk till dawn,
In the melody's arms until we're reborn.
For in the night, love finds its ground,
A serenade for dreams unbound.

Whispers of the Night's Gentle Embrace

In the stillness deep, a secret sigh,
Whispers of the night, softly drift by.
Beneath the stars, where shadows creep,
The heart's desires gently leap.

Moonlight spills like a silken thread,
Weaving stories of the things unsaid.
With every breath, a promise made,
In the gentle embrace where doubts fade.

The stars are eyes that watch and gleam,
In their brilliance, we craft our dream.
Time slows down as silence reigns,
In the night's embrace, love breaks chains.

As echoes linger, soft and clear,
Whispers of longing, holding dear.
In every heartbeat, the world's a stage,
Lost in the beauty of the night's page.

So close your eyes and feel the grace,
Of night's gentle arms, a warm embrace.
For in this moment, we find our place,
In whispers woven, as hearts interlace.

Whispers of Enchanted Sighs

In twilight's grasp, the shadows play,
Soft whispers drift, then fade away.
Among the trees where secrets hide,
The heartbeats echo, side by side.

A flicker of light, a fleeting glance,
In every breeze, a hidden dance.
The world holds magic, if one believes,
In every sigh that the night conceives.

With every leaf that gently sways,
The melody of forgotten days.
A gentle hum, a soft embrace,
Transported to a timeless place.

As starlit dreams begin to weave,
In whispered tones, we dare to grieve.
Yet every sorrow, every tear,
Brings forth a joy that draws us near.

The night's caress, a soothing balm,
In every note, a leash of calm.
United here, our spirits fly,
In whispers sweet, we learn to sigh.

Echoes Beneath the Moonlit Glade

Beneath the moon's soft silver glow,
The whispering winds begin to flow.
In every shadow, dreams unite,
We chase the echoes of the night.

A quiet song from the willow's bough,
Promises of magic—here and now.
Time holds still, yet moments blend,
In moonlit glades where heartbeats mend.

The hoot of owls, a haunting call,
Reveals the secrets held by all.
With bated breath, we wander still,
In harmony with nature's will.

Among the ferns, the fairies play,
Their laughter brightens darkened way.
With twinkles in their eyes of dew,
They lead us forth, our spirits new.

As dawn approaches, colors bloom,
We welcome in the sun's warm room.
Yet in our hearts, the echoes stay,
Of whispers shared beneath the sway.

Secrets Linger in the Moss

In the forest deep, where shadows lie,
Secrets linger, as time goes by.
Mossy carpets where dreamers tread,
In twilight's glow, all fears are shed.

A gentle touch of nature's breath,
Awakens life, defying death.
The murmurs of roots beneath the ground,
In every whisper, a tale is found.

Ferns unfurl like stories untold,
Embracing the warmth from days of old.
With every step, we pause and seek,
The hidden lessons, wise and meek.

The brook babbles soft, a soothing sound,
In harmony with the life around.
As twilight dims, our hearts alight,
In dreams woven from the night.

So let us wander, hand in hand,
Through mossy realms of this enchanted land.
For in the secrets that the wild imparts,
We find the magic that fills our hearts.

Reveries Among the Starlit Meadows

In fields aglow with starlit dreams,
Where moonlight shimmers and softly beams.
Each blossom sways in gentle sighs,
As whispers weave through endless skies.

The nightingale sings a lullaby,
While cosmic dances light the sky.
In midnight's realm, time stands still,
Awakening echoes of our will.

Each glimmering star tells stories old,
Of lovers lost and treasures bold.
With hope held high, we take our flight,
Through reveries that linger bright.

Among the meadows, feelings bloom,
In fragrant air, as dreams resume.
The world expands, our spirits soar,
In twilight's breath, we seek for more.

So let us chase the starlit ways,
And lose ourselves in moonlit plays.
For in this dance beneath the light,
We find our joy, our hearts ignite.

Fragments of a Celestial Lament

In twilight's hush, the stars descend,
Whispers of hopes that time can't fend.
A ghostly waltz upon the night,
Tales of lost dreams take their flight.

The moonlight weaves through shadows cast,
Each twinkle holds a story fast.
A symphony of hearts that sigh,
Fragments of wishes drifting by.

On cloudy shores where silence sleeps,
Memory's touch in darkness creeps.
Soft echoes of a love now still,
Captured in time, an endless thrill.

O, hear the nightingale's sweet song,
In the deep woods where dreams belong.
A melody for the lost and gone,
In the stillness, they linger on.

With every tear the cosmos weeps,
In starlit pools, the heartache keeps.
Fragments swirling, the stories blend,
A celestial lament that will not end.

Traces of Laughter on the Autumn Breeze

Leaves pirouette on a crisp, cool day,
Whispers of laughter in the sun's ray.
A giggle dances through trees that sway,
As autumn weaves magic in child's play.

Pumpkins aglow with a golden grin,
Frolicking spirits where tales begin.
Nature's canvas, a painting bold,
With stories of joy, long to be told.

Crisp apples crunch underfoot with cheer,
As laughter lingers ever near.
The air, sweetened with hints of spice,
Enfolding hearts with warmth so nice.

Children chase shadows on faded grass,
With every giggle, the moments pass.
Memories etched in the amber hue,
Traces of laughter, forever true.

Oh, joyous breeze, carry me along,
To where all souls in harmony throng.
In the embrace of this fleeting dance,
Traces of laughter, a timeless romance.

Glimmers of Magic in Still Waters

In the still pond where the lilies bloom,
Ripples whisper beneath the moon.
Glimmers of magic shimmer and weave,
A tapestry of dreams that cleave.

The water's eyes reflect the sky,
Carrying secrets that float on by.
In every glimmer, a story unfolds,
Of enchanted nights and heroes bold.

Beneath the surface, shadows play,
A dance of spirits that long to stay.
Each flicker a promise, a soft embrace,
In the stillness, they find their place.

Moonbeams shimmer, casting their light,
On whispered wishes that take flight.
With every ripple, a spell is cast,
Binding the present with the past.

Glimmers of magic, like stars on the brink,
In the tranquil waters where dreamers think.
Hold tight to the whispers, the stories to share,
In the heart of the quiet, magic lingers there.

Echoing Footfalls in the Fairy Ring

In the heart of the woods, where shadows fall,
Echoing footfalls, a haunting call.
Around the circle where fairies play,
Magic awakens at the end of day.

Soft whispers lilt through the emerald leaves,
Carried by wind, a tale that weaves.
With every heartbeat, the forest sighs,
Under the gaze of starlit skies.

Mossy stones cradle dreams of old,
In the fairy ring where legends are told.
Each footprint left a story to bind,
A journey of hearts eternally kind.

Beneath the boughs, where time stands still,
Echoes of laughter, a sweet thrill.
In flickering light, the dancers spin,
Harmony rising from deep within.

O, nocturnal blooms, your magic flare,
In this realm where all is fair.
Footfalls echo in twilight's song,
In the fairy ring, where we belong.

Lament of the Sylvan Spirits

In shadows deep where willows weep,
The spirits sigh their secrets keep.
They wander lost in twilight's glow,
For fleeting dreams that won't let go.

Their whispers dance on autumn's breath,
Of love long gone, and silent death.
They weave their tales in ancient trees,
With ghostly voices on the breeze.

In moonlit glades where heartbeats fade,
They chant lost songs in twilight's shade.
Yet through the pain, a beauty flows,
Of life and loss that time bestows.

They paint the night with silver light,
A tapestry of lost delight.
With every tear, a memory grows,
In harmony, their sorrow flows.

So heed the call of forest fair,
Within their hearts, magic lies bare.
In solemn woods where shadows lie,
The spirits weep, yet never die.

Gentle Murmurs of the Woodland

In quiet glades, the whispers sigh,
As eager leaves in breezes lie.
The woodland breathes in tranquil tones,
With secrets spoken through the stones.

The brooklet sings a merry tune,
Beneath the gaze of watchful moon.
It dances forth with laughter bright,
A gentle joy in soft moonlight.

In every rustle, every sound,
The magic of the wild is found.
Where fireflies twinkle, stars descend,
The woodland holds a love to lend.

With fragrant blooms and mossy beds,
The forest weaves its dreams in threads.
In every shadow, stories laced,
The gentle heart of earth embraced.

So walk the path where silence dwells,
And listen close to nature's spells.
For every sigh, a promise grows,
In woodland's heart, the magic flows.

Reflections in the Faery Stream

Beneath the boughs, the waters gleam,
Where faeries dance and shadows dream.
Their laughter trickles with the flow,
In sparkling hues of sunlit glow.

Each ripple tells of tales once spun,
In realms where time is set to run.
The faery stream, a silver thread,
Where wishes linger, hopes are fed.

Upon the surface, starlight plays,
In whispered notes of twilight's praise.
Reflections deep of love and loss,
In every swirl, a tempest toss.

Such magic born of whispered sighs,
In pools where moonlight softly lies.
They weave illusions, soft and bright,
A tapestry of pure delight.

So catch a glimpse as waters flow,
Of dreams and wishes yet to know.
In faery streams, let your heart scheme,
For life's a wondrous, fleeting dream.

Songs of the Fauna Forgotten

In wooded realms where shadows glide,
The fauna hum their songs of pride.
A melody of earth and sky,
In quiet spaces where spirits fly.

Each rustle brings a symphony,
Of life and love in harmony.
The creatures sing of days gone by,
In twilight's hush, a soft goodbye.

The trees bear witness to their song,
In every note, where they belong.
With tales of strength and gentle grace,
They shine in sorrow, sweet embrace.

Through tangled roots and leafy lanes,
Their harmony in joy remains.
In fleeting moments, echoes blend,
Of faunas' tunes that never end.

So lend your ear to nature's choir,
And feel the beat of hearts on fire.
In every whisper, soft and clear,
The songs of old will always hear.

Shadows Danced with Dreaming Leaves

In whispering woods where shadows play,
The leaves come alive, a lively ballet.
They twirl and they twist in twilight's embrace,
Casting soft secrets, lost in their grace.

The moon peeks through, with a silvery grin,
A guardian of dreams where the stories begin.
Each rustle of branches, each sigh in the night,
Tells tales of enchantment, of magic and light.

The starlit sky, a tapestry spun,
Weaves whispers of hope, what shadows have done.
In the hush of the eve, when the world holds its breath,
Lives a dance with the dusk, a waltz with sweet death.

With laughter and joy, the night birds alight,
As shadows embrace the warm kiss of night.
They sway with the magic, they laugh with the wind,
In the heart of the forest, where dreams never end.

So linger a while, where the shadows do dwell,
In the land of the leaves, there's a beautiful spell.
For those who believe in the songs of the trees,
Will find in the darkness their yearning hearts' pleas.

Melodies of Forgotten Realms

In corners of time, where memories hide,
Whispering winds tell of realms far and wide.
Each rustle of pages from books long since read,
Carries melodies sweet, softly spinning their thread.

The echo of laughter from children at play,
Dances through shadows, then gently drifts away.
In the flicker of candles, old stories ignite,
Turning the darkness to shimmering light.

With a quill dipped in starlight, we wander and dream,
Each word a new journey, each page a new theme.
From wizards and witches to creatures so rare,
Melodies linger, rich in the air.

Through valleys of silence, through mountains of night,
Magic reminds us that hope is in sight.
For every fairytale spun with delight,
Has roots in the echoes that shimmer so bright.

So listen, dear traveler, let your heart soar,
For in forgotten realms, there's always more.
With each turn of the page, let new worlds unfold,
In melodies old, new adventures are told.

Glistening Dreams on Twilight's Edge

On twilight's edge where the day softly sighs,
Glistening dreams weave through indigo skies.
The stars shimmer gently, like whispers of light,
Igniting the night with their magical sight.

In gardens of wonder, where wishes take flight,
The flowers are painted with colors so bright.
Each petal a promise, each fragrance a song,
In the stillness of dusk, where the heart can belong.

Beneath the soft glow of a dreaming moon's glow,
The trees tell their secrets, the rivers they flow.
With a flick of the wind, stories twirl and spin,
In the dance of the dusk, new adventures begin.

The shadows embrace as the world starts to fade,
While stardust cascades in this twilight parade.
Hold fast to your dreams, let your spirit roam free,
For glistening dreams hold the key to the sea.

So breathe in the magic that lingers around,
In every soft whisper, in every sweet sound.
For on twilight's edge, where the day meets the night,
Glistening dreams spark, igniting our flight.

Remnants of a Fable's Breath

Amidst the tall tales where heroes roam free,
Lies the whisper of fables, a soft memory.
In echoes of laughter and shadows of fear,
The remnants of stories still linger quite near.

Through forests enchanted, where echoes entwine,
The heartbeat of worlds, in rhythm divine.
Each leaf has a tale, each breeze carries lore,
As the past gently beckons, forevermore.

With ink from the starlight and pages of dreams,
The fabric of myth is not all what it seems.
For within every story that's told with great flair,
Lives the remnants of whispers, a magic laid bare.

So gather the fragments of those who have passed,
Through the corridors of time, their shadows are cast.
Remember their journeys, their laughter, their sighs,
For remnants of fables are never goodbyes.

In the heart of the night, let your spirit take flight,
For the breath of a fable can guide you through night.
With every tale woven, let truth softly cling,
To the remnants of dreams that the nightbirds still sing.

Sighs of the Dew-Kissed Morning

Morning breaks with gentle grace,
Dew-kissed petals smile and sway.
Whispers dance in soft embrace,
Sunbeams weave through skies of grey.

Each breath holds a secret song,
Nature murmurs, fresh and clear.
With every moment, we belong,
To the magic lingering near.

Clouds like cotton begin to part,
Revealing dreams above the hill.
The world awakes, a tender heart,
Embracing daylight's gentle thrill.

Birds take flight in joyful cheer,
Notes of melody fill the air.
All at once, the day draws near,
Wrapped in sunlight, soft and rare.

In this silence, time stands still,
With every dewdrop, hope restored.
The morning breathes, a quiet thrill,
In nature's love, we are adored.

Legends Amongst the Ferns

Whispers of tales in shadows lie,
Beneath the ferns, where secrets grow.
Ancient spirits linger nigh,
Guardians of the tales we know.

In emerald cloaks, they weave their lore,
Of brave knights and whispered doom.
Through tangled roots, their voices soar,
Breathing life into the gloom.

Underneath the starlit gaze,
Echoes of laughter fill the night.
Timeless dreams and starlit days,
Awaken in the moon's soft light.

A world where magic holds its reign,
And every fern has stories to tell.
Through enchanted woods, we walk again,
In a realm of myst'ry, cast a spell.

So listen close, dear wanderer,
To the legends that come alive.
In nature's arms, we stir the stir,
And through the ferns, our spirits thrive.

Twilight's Heartbeat in the Air

When twilight kisses day goodbye,
The sky blushes with hues untold.
Stars begin to wink and sigh,
As the evening's dreams unfold.

In shadows deep, the fireflies gleam,
A dance of lights on whispered breeze.
Each flicker holds a secret dream,
In twilight's arms, we find our ease.

The world transforms with gentle grace,
Soft whispers rise from distant glens.
In this serene, enchanted space,
All worry fades, as peace descends.

Night's breath weaves a soothing spell,
Crickets sing their lullaby sweet.
In twilight's glow we know so well,
Each heartbeat mirrors the night's beat.

As shadows dance and stars ignite,
We lose ourselves in twilight's song.
With every moment cloaked in light,
We find a place where we belong.

The Enchantment of Forgotten Songs

In hushed corners of the mind,
Old melodies begin to play.
Each note a treasure left behind,
Whispers of a bygone day.

Ancient echoes softly call,
From dusty shelves where dreams reside.
Time shall never let them fall,
In memory's arms, they gently hide.

Like leaves that dance on silken air,
The tunes resound, a gentle tune.
With every breath, a fragrant prayer,
Beneath the watchful gaze of moon.

So gather close, dear hearts, and hear,
The songs that linger, sweet and light.
In every whisper, cast aside fear,
For music blooms within the night.

Binding hearts across the years,
The magic of our past, alive.
In melodies, dissolve your fears,
And in forgotten songs, we thrive.

Beneath the Gnarled Roots of Time

Beneath the gnarled roots of time,
Forgotten whispers softly chime.
In shadows deep, where secrets lie,
The ancient trees stand strong and spry.

Their branches weave a tale so old,
Of mysteries wrapped in green and gold.
With every rustle, a story sways,
In silence cast, through countless days.

The earth's embrace, a gentle sigh,
As seasons pass, the stars drift by.
The past and present intertwine,
Beneath the gnarled roots of time.

And though the ages may seem vast,
Each moment holds the echoes cast.
In every knot, a dream preserved,
With nature's hand, the truth observed.

Illusions in the Breath of Dawn

Illusions dance in morning's light,
With whispers soft, they take their flight.
The dew-kissed grass, a canvas bright,
Where dreams awaken from the night.

Each ray of sun, a brush of gold,
Paints stories new, yet untold.
In shadows deep, the secrets spin,
As day unfolds, their tales begin.

The quiet moments linger near,
As dawn reveals what was unclear.
With every breath, the world renews,
Illusions shift in vibrant hues.

The horizon blushes, bathed in fire,
While hearts ignite with pure desire.
Each passing second, a fleeting grace,
In the breath of dawn, we find our place.

Lost Tales on the Degraded Path

On the degraded path we tread,
Lost tales linger in our head.
With every step, a memory frays,
As shadows dance in misty haze.

Forgotten whispers brush the ground,
In the silence, stories bound.
Each fading footprint tells its fate,
Of dreams and hopes, both small and great.

Among the weeds, the remnants sigh,
Of laughter shared and sweet goodbye.
And though the road may twist and bend,
These tales will echo, never end.

For every turn holds what was lost,
The bridge of time, no matter the cost.
In tangled roots and weathered stone,
The spirit of the past is known.

Reverberations of Light Through the Canopy

Reverberations of light cascade,
Through the canopy, shadows laid.
Beneath the boughs, the world confined,
Yet in that space, the heart can find.

The sunbeams dance with vibrant grace,
Illuminating time and space.
Where leaves catch whispers from above,
In nature's song, we find our love.

Each flicker tells a tale anew,
Of past and present intertwined too.
In tangled branches, hope takes flight,
Reverberations of purest light.

As daylight wanes and shadows grow,
The magic lingers, soft and slow.
In the embrace of twilight's hand,
The light will guide us through this land.

Whispers in the Enchanted Glade

In the glade where shadows weave,
Softly hums the evening breeze.
Secrets dance on mossy leaves,
Underneath the ancient trees.

Twinkling lights like fireflies,
Guide the wanderers who roam.
With each step, a magic sighs,
In this secret forest home.

Voices whisper tales of yore,
Of wizards, charms, and mystic rites.
Echoes linger evermore,
Underneath the starry nights.

Footsteps trace the path of dreams,
Where the moonlight softly spills.
Each shadow with its secrets gleams,
Filling hearts with wonder's thrills.

So linger here, let time stand still,
In the glade that time forgot.
Where dreams awaken, hearts can fill,
In this world of magic wrought.

Moonlit Echoes of Forgotten Dreams

Underneath the silver glow,
Whispers float on tranquil air.
Long-lost wishes ebb and flow,
Dancing lightly without care.

Stars above begin to hum,
Echoes of the dreams once dreamed.
In the night, these visions come,
In the quiet, softly streamed.

Each heartbeat sings a lullaby,
Calling forth what once was known.
In the stillness, secrets lie,
Waiting to be heard, not shown.

Through the shadows, tales arise,
Of hopes and fears that sway like trees.
With moonlit beams that mesmerize,
Unlocking hearts with gentle ease.

So take a breath and close your eyes,
Let memories entwine and gleam.
In the night, our spirits rise,
Lost forever in a dream.

A Dance Beneath the Gossamer Veil

In the twilight's soft embrace,
Creatures twirl beneath the sky.
Gossamer threads weave their grace,
As the stars begin to fly.

Whispers lift on fragrant air,
Songs of wonders lost in time.
Every heartbeat holds a prayer,
As they perform, so sweet, so prime.

Footsteps echo on the ground,
With two hearts lost in the throng.
In this dance, a love is found,
As the night hums its sweet song.

Twinkling lights swirl all around,
Drawing us into the dream.
In this moment, love unbound,
A perfect, shimmering theme.

So let us dance, both brave and free,
Underneath the moonlit veil.
In the night, just you and me,
In this magic, we shall sail.

Secrets of the Twilit Meadow

In the meadow, whispers sigh,
Secrets linger, soft and clear.
Beneath the fading twilight sky,
Echoes of the past draw near.

Crickets chirp a gentle tune,
As fireflies twinkle on cue.
Beneath the watchful crescent moon,
The night reveals its hidden view.

Every blade of grass knows tales,
Of lovers and of dreams once spun.
In the quiet, magic prevails,
As day gives way to night begun.

Through the shadows, spirits roam,
Guardians of this sacred ground.
In this space, we find our home,
Where ancient magic can be found.

So wander here, let stories grow,
In the twilight's golden breath.
In this meadow, let love flow,
Embracing life beyond our death.

Celestial Whispers and Gilded Dreams

In the hush of twilight's embrace,
Stars twinkle like secrets of old,
Whispers dance through the wisp of air,
Each one a story waiting to unfold.

Moonbeams caress the slumbering earth,
Casting shadows where dreams take wing,
Gilded hopes in the night do laugh,
While the cosmos hums, sweetly they sing.

Among the clouds, wishes ascend,
Caught in the weave of the starry night,
Every heartbeat pulses with wonder,
A tapestry glimmers, pure and bright.

In this realm where wishes convene,
A magical world softly gleams,
Celestial wonders ignite the heart,
As we journey through gilded dreams.

So hush now, let silence befriend,
The lull of night shall not betray,
For in the dreams where stardust swirls,
Awaits the dawn of a brand new day.

Leafy Secrets in the Silent Wood

In a forest where shadows creep,
Leaves murmur tales of ancient lore,
Wandering paths of moss and stone,
Glimmers of magic forevermore.

Beneath the boughs where silence reigns,
Whispers of faeries softly play,
Each rustling leaf a hidden thought,
Secrets echo, then drift away.

Creeping ivy, bold and green,
Hides the entrance to realms unknown,
With every step, the world transforms,
In the wood where the wild winds moan.

Moonlight weaves through branches bare,
A silver thread in the quiet night,
Entwined with dreams of those who dare,
To seek the truth in fading light.

So linger, dear heart, in this glade,
Where leafy secrets will reveal,
For in the embrace of the silent wood,
The magic of nature is surreal.

Unspoken Wishes on the Breath of Night

As shadows draw across the land,
Unspoken wishes float on air,
Announcing hopes that softly float,
In the stillness, hearts lay bare.

Each breath a promise, fleeting fast,
Wrapped in the cloak of the soft dark,
Stars shimmer sweetly in their gaze,
Awaiting the spark of a whispered remark.

Moonlit pathways, secrets roam,
Where dreams and reality intertwine,
In the hush of night, we hold our breath,
As wishes hang like grapes on the vine.

A breeze stirs softly, gently sways,
Carrying thoughts that never died,
In the silence of twilight's cloak,
Unspoken wishes are our guide.

So close your eyes, and let them soar,
On arcs of stardust, high and free,
For in the night, our dreams await,
To blossom where the heart can see.

Joys of the Firefly's Flight

In twilight fields where shadows dance,
Fireflies weave a tapestry bright,
They flicker like stars that have fallen,
Bringing joy through the softening night.

They twirl and glide with graceful ease,
A ballet of light in the cool air,
Each glow a flicker of fleeting bliss,
In the symphony of evening's glare.

Children laugh, capturing dreams,
As the night holds its magic tight,
With every spark, a memory made,
In the warm embrace of the starry night.

These tiny lanterns, bold and free,
Guide wanderers lost in the dark,
In their gentle glow, we find our way,
A spark of joy, a glowing arc.

So gather close, let the magic in,
For fireflies hold a wondrous sight,
In their flight, we find our hearts,
The joys of the firefly's flight.

Hope Flickers in the Glade

In the heart of the woods, whispers grow,
Gentle breezes through branches flow.
A flicker of light where shadows weave,
Promises bloom, for those who believe.

The leaves softly chatter, secrets unfold,
Tales of the brave, of legends retold.
Every heartbeat of nature sings,
In the glade, hope takes wings.

With lanterns of fireflies dancing bright,
Guiding the lost through the quiet night.
With courage wrapped in a silken thread,
The spirit of wonder shall never be dead.

Among blossoms that shimmer with dew,
Magic awakens, both ancient and new.
A flicker of warmth in the chill of despair,
In the glade, love lingers with care.

So linger a while, let your hopes grow,
In the heartbeat of nature, let the light glow.
For those who look closely, joy shall abide,
In the glade where the flicker of hope resides.

The Dance of Light in the Pitch of Night

When shadows stretch wide, and silence reigns,
The stars weave their spells in silvery chains.
With a sparkle of dreams that flicker and bend,
The dance of light begins without end.

Moonbeams pirouette on the velvet ground,
Whispers of magic, a soft, soothing sound.
In the stillness where night creatures glide,
The secrets of worlds intertwine and collide.

The laughter of fireflies, a symphony sweet,
Illuminates paths where the lost souls meet.
Each glimmer of starlight, a story to tell,
Of hopes shining brightly, casting their spell.

In the distance, the echoes of old lullabies,
Bring comfort to dreamers and long-faded sighs.
With every twinkle, a promise unfolds,
In the dance of the night, a magic that holds.

So wait for the moment, let stillness ignite,
The dance of you and the stars in the night.
For beneath the vast heavens, we all take flight,
In a world that is woven with dreams filled with light.

Gentle Rain on the Fae's Dream

A soft patter whispers on petals so fair,
Carrying secrets on the cool breeze of air.
Gentle rain falls on a slumbering glade,
Awakening dreams where magic was laid.

Each droplet a story that dances in flight,
Kisses of moisture in shadow and light.
As the flowers sway and the leaves gently sigh,
In sorrow or joy, their spirits fly high.

The fae weave their laughter, like silk in the mist,
Beneath the soft rhythm of raindrops they twist.
With every soft splash, the earth breathes anew,
In the heart of the forest, where dreams come true.

As twilight descends, the colors ignite,
A tapestry woven from day into night.
For the gentle rain holds a magic unseen,
In the realm of the fae, where wonders convene.

So let the world hush, let your heart feel the pull,
Of whispers and wishes where magic is full.
For in every droplet, a dream shall remain,
In the soft, gentle touch of the fae's sweet rain.

Visions in the Misty Haze

In the morning's embrace, the world holds its breath,
Veiled in the haze of a dreamy caress.
Mysteries linger where shadows take flight,
In whispers of visions, both fragile and bright.

The sunrise unveils a tapestry spun,
Of shimmering colors, a day just begun.
Faint echoes of laughter drift through the air,
As the mist weaves its magic, ethereal and rare.

Through the veil, see the figures that dance,
The fleeting enchantments that spark the romance.
In the hush of the morn, where the world calls your name,

Every heartbeat a promise, igniting the flame.

For hidden in beauty, the stories expand,
Of dreams that take flight on a soft, whispered strand.
In the magic of twilight, as dusk starts to fade,
The visions awaken from where they were laid.

So journey with wonder, let doubt melt away,
For in the misty haze, your heart shall display.
In the facets of dreams, with each step you take,
The path of the future begins with the wake.

Starlit Paths in Hidden Realms

Beneath the silver glow of night,
Wanderers tread where shadows light.
Secrets whisper on the breeze,
In hidden realms, with ancient trees.

Each step unveils a tale untold,
Of dreams and myths from days of old.
In starlit paths, our hearts align,
With fate entwined, like roots of vine.

A melody of crickets hums,
Where time stands still, and magic comes.
With every breath, the magic swells,
In places where the wonder dwells.

The moonlight dances on the brook,
In glades where ancient spirits look.
A tapestry of stars adorns,
The night, as peace and joy is born.

Emberlight and Elven Lullabies

In forests deep where shadows play,
The elven songs drift far away.
With emberlight on emerald ground,
An echo of their grace is found.

Crickets chirp a soothing tune,
Beneath the watchful, gentle moon.
Velvet petals in soft bloom,
Enchant the night with sweet perfume.

In twilight's arms, the fables rise,
Of starlit dreams and boundless skies.
Each lullaby a soft embrace,
That lingers on in timeless space.

With silver threads, the night weaves tales,
Of distant lands and whispered gales.
A world where hope and magic blend,
In emberlight, where dreams ascend.

The Lure of Moss-Covered Stones

Beneath the trees where silence reigns,
Moss-covered stones hold ancient claims.
They whisper softly to the stream,
Of stories lost in twilight's dream.

With every step, a secret calls,
Gone are the days when laughter falls.
Each stone a keeper of the past,
In twilight's glow, our journeys cast.

The forest hums with life unseen,
A magic woven into green.
With fingers tracing mossy skin,
We find the worlds that lie within.

The pull of earth, of time's embrace,
An echoed heartbeat, a sacred place.
Where nature girds her ancient throne,
And every stone, a magic stone.

Shadows of the Ancient Grove

In ancient groves where shadows creep,
The spirits dance, the secrets keep.
With twisted branches reaching high,
They hold the whispers of the sky.

In every rustle, tales unfold,
Of hearts entwined and legends bold.
A tapestry of light and shade,
In every corner, dreams are laid.

The air is thick with stories told,
Where time moves slow, and dreams take hold.
A world where magic breathes and sighs,
Beneath the watchful, starry eyes.

So step within this hallowed space,
And find a glimpse of time and grace.
In shadows deep, your heart will know,
The whispers of the ancient grove.

Velvet Skies and Unseen Beings

In twilight's glow, soft whispers weave,
Beneath the velvet skies we grieve.
Stars blink their tales, oh secrets shared,
Unseen beings dance, fate's threads declared.

The night enfolds with silken grace,
Reflecting dreams in a hidden space.
Moonbeams brush the shadows slight,
Illuminating paths in the shrouded night.

Mysteries breathe with each gentle sigh,
As cosmic wonders flutter and fly.
Through softest mists, the echoes call,
In this realm of dreams, we discover all.

Voices of starlight, a lullaby sung,
As ancient hearts beat; new songs are sprung.
A tapestry woven in twilight's embrace,
Unseen beings entwined in sacred space.

With velvet skies, our spirits ignite,
In harmony bound, we find our light.
Together we soar, where shadows dissolve,
In dreams' rich embrace, together we evolve.

Orbweaver's Lament in the Twilight

In the hush of night, a web does gleam,
Crafted of silver, spun from a dream.
The orbweaver sighs, her labor complete,
Under twilight's gaze, a bittersweet beat.

Each thread tells a story of moments now lost,
In the tapestry woven, we pay the cost.
Frost kisses gently the edges so fine,
A lament in the darkness, a fragile line.

Stars pierce the veil, like pearls in the night,
While shadows of memories take wing in flight.
Quiet her heart as the soft winds blow,
Ephemeral echoes of tales long ago.

Every drop of dew, a tear to recall,
The beauty and sorrow in nature's thrall.
With each morning's light, the web fades away,
An orbweaver's sorrow, as night turns to day.

Yet hope lingers on in the dawn's warm embrace,
For new tales emerge in this endless space.
In twilight we weave, forever we'll dream,
With each gentle whisper, a continuous theme.

The Heartbeats of Hidden Glens

In shaded nooks where whispers dwell,
The heartbeats of glens weave a silent spell.
With ancient oaks and streams that glide,
Secrets are kept where shadows abide.

Life dances softly on dewdrop's edge,
Nature's watch falls like a tender pledge.
The song of the lark, a distant refrain,
Echoes through woodlands, joy intertwined with pain.

As sunbeams flicker through emerald leaves,
A tapestry grows where the spirit believes.
The pulse of the earth, in moments so still,
Calls forth the heartbeat, a wondrous thrill.

In hidden glens, the wild blooms bright,
Coloring life in the canvas of night.
Each breath of the glen sings of time's gentle flow,
A symphony played where the wildflowers grow.

As twilight descends, we gather as one,
Beneath the vast skies where our journey begun.
In the heartbeats of glens, we find our way,
In nature's embrace, together we'll stay.

Beneath the Canopy of Stars

Beneath the canopy, starlit and fair,
Whispers of magic hang thick in the air.
Velvet night blankets the world in its grace,
While mystery dances in shadowed embrace.

Each twinkle a story, each spark a delight,
Illuminates dreams in the velvety night.
With eyes turned upward, we breathe in the skies,
Where time unravels as wonder replies.

The moon guides our hearts like a lantern afloat,
Casting soft dreams in a shimmering boat.
In pools of starlight, our spirits we free,
In the vastness of night, together to be.

Through soft rustling leaves, the shadows converse,
With secrets of old, and the universe.
In silence we gather, no words left to part,
With the pulse of the cosmos, we weave our heart.

So let us be lost in this celestial waltz,
As the stars bear witness to all our faults.
For beneath the stars, we are daring and true,
In this endless expanse, it's just me and you.

A Glimmer Through the Misty Boughs

In twilight's dance, the shadows play,
A secret world where whispers stray.
The moonlight spills on dew-kissed ground,
As dreams awaken, subtly found.

With every leaf, the stories weave,
Of ancient woods where few believe.
A glimmer laughs beneath the trees,
And beckons those who dare perceive.

The echo of a distant song,
In tangled roots where hearts belong.
A path obscured, yet ever near,
Inviting souls who wish to steer.

Through misty boughs, the night unfolds,
Revealing tales that time upholds.
The fireflies dance like tiny stars,
Guiding lost hearts from near and far.

So linger here where shadows wane,
And find the magic in the rain.
For in this realm where spirits drift,
A glimmer's light becomes a gift.

The Silent Call of the Willow Tree

Beneath the branches, whispers sigh,
The willow beckons, low and high.
With grace it bends to every breeze,
A guardian of gentle ease.

The tales it tells in soft green hues,
Of lovers lost and dreamers' views.
With roots entwined, the earth it knows,
A silent call where fortune flows.

The twilight bathes its weeping form,
In shadows deep, a shelter warm.
Each tear that falls, a wish released,
In every droplet, hope increased.

A secret kept for wandering souls,
The willow wraps them, makes them whole.
With every breath, the past unfolds,
In whispered tones, its heart beholds.

So listen close when night descends,
For in its song, the spirit mends.
The silent call will draw you near,
To find your peace, your purpose clear.

Ethereal Dreams on the Breeze

In moonlit hours, the dreams take flight,
On gentle winds, through velvet night.
They carry whispers from afar,
A dance of hopes, a silver spar.

With every sigh, the shadows play,
As starlit thoughts drift far away.
A tapestry of moments bright,
Ethereal dreams bathe in soft light.

The heart unbinds its heavy chains,
In the embrace of soft refrains.
Each slumber's breath, a lullaby,
In realms where lost wishes fly.

So close your eyes and drift along,
To where the night sings its sweet song.
For in this world, your spirit gleams,
A voyage born from whispered dreams.

In gentle currents, hope will swirl,
Embracing you in twilight's pearl.
So take the leap, let go your fears,
And find your laughter through the years.

A Serenade for the Lost Wanderer

In twilight's hush, a song takes flight,
For souls adrift in search of light.
With every step, the echoes call,
A serenade for one and all.

The winding path, it bends and breaks,
Yet every heart, a journey makes.
In forest depths or mountain high,
The lost shall find where dreams comply.

Beside the streams where wishes swim,
A lullaby from nature's rim.
The stars above begin to shine,
A guiding light, the world divine.

So gather strength from shadows cast,
For every trial won't be the last.
With open arms, embrace the night,
A serenade to find your light.

For in the whispers of the trees,
A haunting note that drifts with ease.
The lost wanderer shall come to see,
That home resides in their own heart's plea.

The Murmuring Preludes of Enchantment

In twilight's glow, the whispers rise,
Secrets nestled beneath the skies.
A flicker of magic in the air,
Where dreams are spun with utmost care.

The moonlight weaves a silken thread,
Guiding the heart where hopes are fed.
With every note, a story starts,
Echoing softly, enchanting hearts.

Through ancient woods, the shadows play,
As starlit dreams flutter and sway.
Each step unveils a tale untold,
In whispers of silver and threads of gold.

With laughter twinkling in the breeze,
The night unfolds, a realm of ease.
As starlings sing, in gentle streams,
We dance together, lost in dreams.

A tapestry woven with moments bright,
Filling the soul with pure delight.
Beneath the shimmer of the vast expanse,
Join in the murmuring, a sacred dance.

Shadows Cast by Flickering Flames

In the hearth's glow, the shadows leap,
Whispers of stories buried deep.
With every flicker, the past ignites,
Casting long tales in the still of nights.

The glow of embers, warm and bright,
Holds close the secrets of the night.
Figures twist and turn with glee,
In the dance of flames, wild and free.

Chasing away the lurking dread,
Each spark a promise, softly spread.
A sanctuary made of light,
Where hope ignites in fear's dark flight.

Celestial fables fed by dreams,
Rippling through the fire's seams.
Ancestors whisper through the glow,
In shadows cast, their spirits flow.

So gather close, let laughter soar,
In flickering light, forevermore.
With every flame, our hearts entwined,
In shadows cast, true joys we'll find.

Traces of Wonder Through the Ferns

In emerald cloaks, the ferns arise,
Where sunlight dances, softly sighs.
Each leaf a cradle for tales untold,
Whispers of wonder in shades of gold.

Beneath the fronds, a secret path,
Where shadows play and giggles laugh.
Step lightly here, where enchantments cling,
And nature hums her timeless song to sing.

With every breeze, the forest speaks,
A language found in rustling leaks.
A chorus rising, sweet and clear,
In traces of wonder, we hold dear.

Each petal painted in a hue,
Draws us near to the world anew.
Through tangled roots and winding trails,
The magic whispers as nature prevails.

So wander deep where ferns embrace,
And find the beauty in this place.
For every step in wonder's name,
Unveils the heart of the wild's great game.

The Ethereal Dance of Whispering Leaves

In golden light, the leaves shall play,
Softly murmuring the dreams of day.
With every flutter, secrets shared,
An ethereal dance, nature's unpaired.

From ancient boughs, the stories flow,
Each twist and turn, they freely show.
In the gentle wind, their laughter sings,
A symphony born on whispered wings.

As shadows waltz in twilight's grace,
The leaves invite us to embrace.
In nature's pulse, alive with dreams,
Find magic weaved in delicate seams.

The rustle speaks of timeless lore,
Of hearts entwined on nature's floor.
With every breeze, a tale we weave,
In the ethereal dance of whispering leaves.

So pause a moment, breathe it in,
Where nature grins and life begins.
For in this dance, so pure and free,
Lies the essence of you and me.

Twilight's Embrace in Emerald Hollow

In emerald woods, the shadows play,
As twilight whispers, night meets day.
The fireflies dance, their lights aglow,
In secret glades where soft winds blow.

Beneath the boughs, the silence hums,
A symphony of gentle drums.
The crescent moon begins to rise,
Silver glimmers in darkened skies.

Ancient trees in stillness sway,
Sharing secrets of yesterday.
The deer tread softly, hearts aligned,
In twilight's grasp, their truths entwined.

With every breath, enchantments weave,
In magic's hold, we can believe.
The echoes of a world unseen,
Twilight's embrace, serene and keen.

Enigma in the Misty Glen

In a glen where shadows stir,
Mysterious fogs begin to blur.
Voices whisper through the haze,
Kept in secrets of ancient ways.

The willows weep, their branches low,
Tales of time that ebb and flow.
A subtle breeze carries the sound,
Of enchantments waiting to be found.

Glimmers hide in cloaks of gray,
Guiding wanderers who stray.
With every step, the mystery grows,
Entwined within the glen's soft prose.

In each shadow, a story sleeps,
In the mist, the promise keeps.
A heartbeats echo, wild and free,
In a world that longs to flee.

As darkness falls, the night unfurls,
Embracing dreams and magic swirls.
In this glen, the soul finds peace,
An enigma where troubles cease.

Lullabies of the Woodland Spirits

In the heart of woods, where echo sings,
Woodland spirits weave their strings.
Gentle whispers on leafy sighs,
Lullabies beneath soft, starlit skies.

Frogs croak sweetly, crickets hum,
Nature's choir in evening's drum.
Mossy beds where dreams reside,
In twilight's arms, we're bathed in tide.

Fairies flit with candlelight,
Guiding dreams through shimmering night.
Each note a wish, each breath a prayer,
In this haven, free from despair.

With every rustle, worries cease,
In woodland's arms, we find our peace.
The forest cradles hearts as one,
In lullabies until the dawn.

So close your eyes and softly dream,
In nature's hold, let your thoughts stream.
The songs of spirits weave their might,
Lullabies of love throughout the night.

Veils of Memory in the Faded Vale

In the vale where echoes dwell,
Veils of memory spin their spell.
Lost in whispers of the past,
In fading light, shadows are cast.

Time-worn paths of overgrown trails,
Guard the tales that time unveils.
With every step, the stories unfold,
In hidden corners, dreams retold.

Each leaf a witness, each stone a sage,
Turning whispers from page to page.
In the silence, the heartbeats pause,
Remembering love without a cause.

In twilight's glow, the vale reveals,
The weight of time that softly heals.
Collecting fragments, we weave them tight,
In memory's veil, a tapestry bright.

Embrace the stillness, let it flow,
In the faded vale, let memories grow.
With every breath, the past aligns,
In twilight's arms, our spirit shines.

www.ingramcontent.com/pod-product-compliance
Lightning Source LLC
Chambersburg PA
CBHW051940220125
20712CB00003B/57